Giggling and with the Groundhogs of Happy Town

STORY FOUR

PAT M. MOORE

ISBN: 978-1-960147-69-1

Dedication

To my writer friends:

Anne, Jan, Jimmie, Joy, Judy, Kristin, Tanya,
Margaret, Mary B., Mary T., Sharon, and Urmilla.

You make me giggle.
You also help to keep me well-grounded.
Thank you for listening to my stories.
Thanks, too, for your wise insights,
comments, and suggestions.
I am grateful for our friendships.

How much wood could a woodchuck chuck
if a woodchuck could chuck wood?

This group of words is hard to say.
It's called a tongue twister.

Say it five times with family or friends —
faster and faster each time.
Soon you'll be talking gibberish and giggling.

Use your super-power mind to create
your own tongue twisters.
This is especially fun on holidays.

I made this one up for Halloween:
*Wanda Woker watched the wicked witch
wash her whiskered kitten.*

And here's a Christmas twister:
The *cheerful kitten chewed on*
chunky chocolate chip Christmas cookies.

I like sharing tongue twisters,
but this book is about groundhogs.
So, we'd better move on.

Do you know that groundhogs and woodchucks
are the same animal?

They're called groundhogs because they live underground and
only come out a couple of times a day in warmer weather.

But why are they called *woodchuck*s?

When English-speaking people first came to our country, they met the Native Americans who lived here.

Native people called groundhogs
wuchaks, woodchooks, and similar names.
When English people said these names,
it sounded like *woodchucks.*
Some people still use this term.

Groundhogs have other names —
whistle pigs and *land beavers* are just two.

They make *whistling* sounds when scared.
Guinea *pigs* are their cousins.
So, they're sometimes called whistle pigs.

And they are known as land beavers,
because they look like *beavers*
but spend most of their time on or under the *land.*

Although they look alike,
beavers and groundhogs are quite different.

Beavers

Can you guess which animal is the groundhog's closest relative? Squirrels!

Groundhogs are bigger than squirrels.
Squirrels have longer, bushier tails.
Otherwise, these cousins are very similar.

Both have brownish-grey or reddish-brown fur,
round heads, little ears, and small dark eyes.
They also have short legs and long claws.
Both can climb trees quickly.

Groundhog   **Squirrel**

Groundhogs sleep underground all winter.
This is called *hibernating*.
Ground squirrels hibernate underground, too.
Other squirrels build tree nests.

The front teeth of these animals never stop growing.

Thankfully, their teeth rub against each other
as they eat, which wears them down.
Eating hard food like nuts also shortens teeth.

Groundhogs like living alone.
At three months old,
they dig new homes and find food for themselves.

This guy has a shovel,
but real groundhogs dig with their claws.

Adult groundhogs are about 2-feet long —
the length of two rulers set side by side.

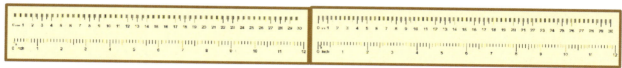

Their average weight is 8-1/2 pounds—
probably not much more than you weighed
when you were born.

Although they're small, they are clever engineers
and create their homes, called *burrows*.

Instead of using wood and bricks,
groundhogs dig homes inside the ground.
Many have summer and winter dwellings.

The summer homes have two or more entrances and exits.
If groundhogs sense danger,
they use these to enter or leave quickly.

Groundhogs dig big holes with tunnels
leading to other holes that are used
as bedrooms and bathrooms.

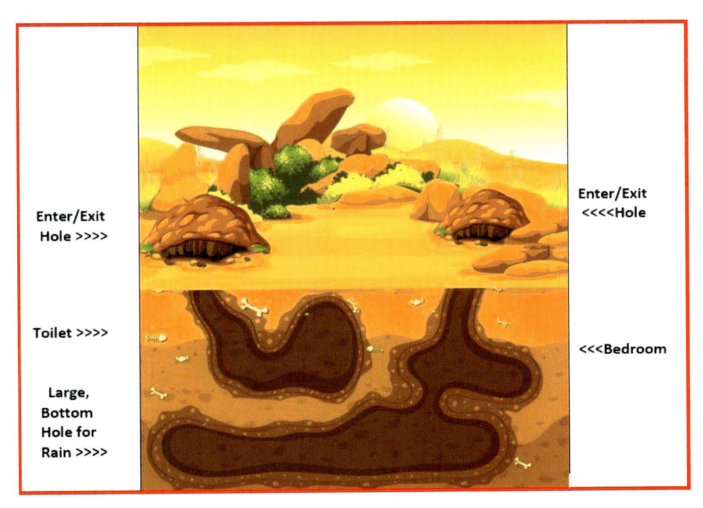

Enter/Exit
Hole >>>>

Toilet >>>>

Large,
Bottom
Hole for
Rain >>>>

Enter/Exit
<<<<Hole

<<<Bedroom

A large hole at the bottom collects rainwater
and keeps the upper levels dry.

Because they dig holes and eat plants,
most farmers don't like groundhogs.

But they can be helpful.
They eat bugs, so fewer insects are around
to bother plants and people.

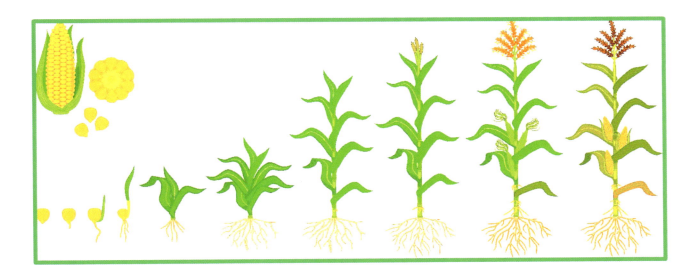

Their digging also helps plant roots breathe.
And it spreads seeds.
Therefore, more plants can grow and mature.

Groundhogs have two layers of fur.
This makes them look bigger than they are.
The top layer is like a raincoat; it keeps them dry.
The bottom one keeps them warm.

They eat plants and nuts, which don't grow in cold weather.
Unlike people, animals can't buy food at a store.
But groundhogs have wise instincts and
can live for 5 months without eating.

They overeat in summer to gain extra weight.
This feeds their bodies while they hibernate.

Sleeping also helps them live without food,
because they use less energy.

While hibernating,
groundhogs wake up about once each week,
use their bathrooms, and then return to sleep.

After long winter naps, the boys wake up first,
go outside, and walk around their *territories*.
These are sections of land
that groundhogs claim for themselves.

Some have larger territories than others.
Most are the size of one or two football fields.

They look for girl-groundhog burrows,
hoping to find girlfriends.
When a boy and girl meet, they get to know each other
by spending time together.

After that, the boys go home.
But they return to their girlfriends in March.
About a month later, the females have babies.

Dad and mom don't live together,
but daddy walks around every day,
ensuring his family is safe.

Some people think groundhogs
can predict if winter will be long or short.

They think Groundhog Day, February 2,
is when boy groundhogs first go outside
after hibernation.

According to these people,
"When February 2nd is sunny,
groundhogs see their shadows, get scared,
and run back into their holes for another 6 weeks.

"This means 6 more weeks of winter.

"But if it's cloudy,
groundhogs don't see their shadows.
They stay outside awhile,
which means spring is coming soon."

Happy Groundhog Day

Groundhogs are miracles of Nature.

Clever and cute, they remind us that animals are special
and among the many gifts, our planet offers.

When you're outside this week, notice the different animals.
Think about their unique habits, beauty, and intelligence.
What can they do that you can't?

Can you fly or catch food with your tongue?
Pay attention.
You'll be surprised how many animals
have superpowers you don't.

Happy Towners like to draw and paint pictures of Nature.

This helps them to better appreciate its wonderfulness.

Why not draw or paint a picture of *your* favorite animal?

When we create pictures of Nature,
we automatically pay more attention.
We get to know our world better.
And this helps our hearts and minds to grow.

On the next nice day, go outside and hug a tree.
Feel the energy that comes from its deep roots,
and moves up to the sky through its branches.

This energy is part of you.
It means that you are never alone, because
you and all living things share the same energy.

If you have enjoyed this book, please consider adding a review on Amazon. Thank You.

About the Author

Pat Moore often thinks about growing up in New Hampshire with seven siblings -- five were younger than her. Those memories have evolved into a lifetime fondness for children.

She has adored being a mother, stepmother, and grandmother. Pat has seven grandchildren, many nieces, nephews, great nieces, and great nephews.

She is writing a series of "Happy Town" books that can guide youngsters (and adults) in learning to think better (happier & wiser) thoughts, acting with love & kindness, and enjoying the magic that surrounds us every day.

Pat has always loved books and writing. She enjoys participating with her friends in book clubs and writer groups.

She holds a BA from the University of Maryland and an MS from George Washington University. She and her husband established PMR Communications Group in 2003. They live in Virginia.

Made in the USA
Middletown, DE
13 March 2024

51340291R00020